Mediterranean Diet Meals Specialties

50 & More Ideas for Mediterranean Meals

Mateo Buscema

TABLE OF CONTENTS

Slim Greek deviled eggs

Only try out this recipe if you are ready to enjoy a finger licking delicious variation with deviled eggs.

They are easy to make yet popular contribution to a brunch of tasty home kitchen.

Ingredients

- 1/8 teaspoon of pepper
- ½ teaspoon of grated lemon zest
- 1/8 teaspoon of salt
- ½ teaspoon of lemon juice
- 6 hard ready boiled large eggs
- 1 teaspoon of oregano
- 3 tablespoons of fatless mayonnaise
- 2 tablespoons of crumbled feta cheese
- Greek olives (optional)

Directions

1. Lengthwise, cut the eggs into half.
2. Completely remove the yolk and put aside the whites and the yolks.
3. Using a large bowl, mash the reserved yolks.

4. Stir in the mayonnaise, oregano, feta, lemon juice, lemon zest, pepper, and salt.
5. Stuff into the egg whites.
6. If desired, garnish with the Greek olives.
7. Let it chill until ready to serve
8. Enjoy

Greek tofu scramble

Ingredients

- 2 tablespoon of nutritional yeast
- juice of ½ lemon
- salt and pepper
- 1 tablespoon of oil
- ¼ small red onion, diced
- 2 cloves garlic, minced
- ½ cup of red bell pepper, diced
- 8 ounces of firm tofu
- 1 handful of fresh spinach
- ¼ cup of fresh basil, chopped
- ¼ teaspoon of salt
- ¼ cup of Kalamata olives, pitted and halved
- 11 teaspoon of tahini paste
- ½ cup of cherry tomatoes, halved

Directions

1. In a small bowl, crumble tofu to the texture of scrambled eggs.
2. Add nutritional yeast, tahini, lemon juice, and salt and keep aside.
3. In a large skillet , heat oil over medium heat.

4. Add onions and sauté for 5 minutes, stirring occasionally.

5. Add bell pepper and garlic and sauté for another 5 minutes until the bell pepper is tender.

6. Stir crumbled tofu and Kalamata olives.

7. Heat all the way through, stirring occasionally.

8. Add spinach and basil.

9. Stir to wilted slightly, reducing to about half its size.

10. Remove from heat and stir in cherry tomatoes.

11. Season with salt and pepper.

12. Serve and enjoy.

Greek veggie tacos

Ingredients

- 6 Kalamata olives
- 2 soft taco shells
- 2 tablespoons of crumbled feta cheese
- 2 tablespoons of hummus
- 2 tablespoons of Greek dressing
- 2 tablespoons of thinly sliced and chopped red onion
- 4 slices of cucumber, quartered
- 1 Roma tomato, cubed
- Leafy green lettuce

Directions

1. Begin by spreading 1 tablespoon of hummus onto each soft taco.
2. Fill tacos with cucumbers together with the tomatoes, red onions, olives and crumbled feta.
3. Top with 1 tablespoon of Greek dressing on each.
4. Serve and enjoy.

Kalamata olive spread

Ingredients

- ½ teaspoon of dried oregano
- ½ cup of pitted Kalamata olives
- 1 teaspoon of red wine vinegar

Directions

1. Use an immersion blender, blend all ingredients together until smooth.
2. Store in a sealed container in the refrigerator.
3. Serve and enjoy.

Pan-seared citrus shrimp

Ingredients

- 1 medium lemon, cut into wedges
- 1 cup of fresh orange juice
- ½ cup of fresh lemon juice
- 5 garlic cloves, minced or pressed
- 3 pounds of medium shrimp, peeled and deveined
- 1 tablespoon of finely chopped red onion
- 1 tablespoon of olive oil
- 1 medium orange, cut into wedges
- Pinch of red pepper flakes
- Freshly ground black pepper and kosher salt
- 1 tablespoon of chopped fresh parsley

Directions

1. In a medium bowl, whisk together the olive oil with orange juice, lemon juice, 2 teaspoons of the parsley, garlic, onion, and pinch of red pepper flakes.
2. Pour the mixture into a large skillet set over medium heat.
3. Bring to a simmer and cook until reduced by half in 8 minutes.
4. Add the shrimp.

5. Season with kosher salt and freshly ground black pepper.
6. Cover let cook until they turn pink in 5 minutes.
7. Top with the remaining parsley
8. Serve and enjoy with orange and lemon slices on the side.

Hummus toast

Making hummus traditionally is a lot fun and tastier yet with no fuss and additional flavors.

This recipe is simply a plain and classic recipe.

Note, the outcome of the recipe should be thick, rich, smooth, and creamy.

Ingredients

- Hot water
- Sumac
- 3 to 4 ice cubes
- ⅓ cup tahini paste
- Early Harvest Greek extra virgin olive oil
- Juice of 1 lemon
- ½ teaspoon of kosher salt
- 3 cups cooked and peeled chickpeas
- 1 to 2 garlic cloves, minced

Directions

1. In a bowl of a food processor, introduce the minced garlic together with the chickpeas.

2. Start to puree until a visible smooth powder like mixture appears.
3. Add the ice cubes, salt, lemon juice, and tahini while the processing is still running.
4. Continue to blend for 4 minutes about.
5. In the event that the thick semi-liquid solution is still too thick, add more water to dilute while the processor is still running.
6. Blend until the solution turns silky smooth.
7. Get a serving bowl, spread in it and then add early harvest extra virgin olive oil with drizzle.
8. Add some chickpeas in the middle.
9. Sprinkle the top with sumac
10. Serve and enjoy with warm pita wedges and other veggies you like.

Foul mudamma recipe

This recipe simply involves stewing broad or fava beans which is seasoned with ground cumin finished with extra virgin olive oil.

The Egyptians love to enjoy it with warm pita bread, fresh veggies, lemon juice and also herbs.

Ingredients

- Diced 1 tomato
- 1 large lemon juice
- Extra virgin olive oil
- ½ cup water
- 1 to 2 hot peppers, chopped
- 2 chopped garlic cloves
- Kosher salt
- 2 cans plain fava beans
- ½ to 1 teaspoon ground cumin
- 1 cup chopped parsley

To Serve

- Sliced cucumbers
- Olives
- Warm pit bread
- Green onions

- Sliced tomatoes

Directions

1. In a saucepan, add ½ cup of water and the fava beans.
2. Warm it over a medium temperature
3. Season it with cumin and kosher salt.
4. Mash the beans.
5. Add hot peppers together with garlic in a mortar and pestle, then smash them.
6. Introduce one lemon juice, stir to blend
7. Over the fava beans, pour the blended hot pepper and garlic sauce.
8. Add a drizzle of extra virgin olive oil and top with diced tomatoes, and chopped parsley.
9. Serve and enjoy with veggies, pitta bread and or olives.

Easy shakshuka recipe

Ingredients

- 2 garlic cloves, peeled, chopped
- 1 large yellow onion, chopped
- Salt and pepper
- ¼ cup chopped fresh mint leaves, 5 grams
- Extra virgin olive oil
- ¼ cup chopped fresh parsley leaves, 5 grams
- 2 green peppers, chopped
- ½ tsp ground cumin
- 6 chopped Vine-ripe tomatoes
- ½ cup tomato sauce
- 1 tsp sweet paprika
- 6 large eggs
- 1 tsp ground coriander
- Pinch red pepper flakes, optional

Directions

1. Start by heating 3 teaspoons of olive oil in a saucepan.
2. Add onions, garlic, spices, pinch salt, pepper and green peppers.
3. Cook while you keep stirring occasionally to soften the veggies for 5 minutes.

4. Introduce the tomatoes and tomato sauce together.
5. Cover to allow it to simmer for 15 minutes.
6. Uncover the content completely to allow it thicken while still cooking.
7. Adjust the seasoning according to the taste.
8. Make 6 indentation preferably using a wooden spoon in the tomato sauce.
9. Break eggs and pour in each of the indentations.
10. Reduce the heat, then completely cover the skillet.
11. Continue to cook on low heat to set the white eggs
12. Uncover and introduce the parsley and mint.
13. Serve with warm pita and or add red pepper if desired.
14. Enjoy

Italian oven roasted vegetables

The Italian roasted vegetable is a Mediterranean Sea diet that is made out of a variety of veggies.

It can be seasoned and using extra virgin olive oil it can be tossed.

This recipe is absolutely gluten free.

Ingredients

- Salt and pepper
- 10-12 large peeled garlic cloves
- 8 baby Bella mushrooms with ends trimmed
- Extra virgin olive oil
- 12 oz. baby potatoes, scrubbed
- 12 oz. Campari tomatoes, grape or cherry tomatoes
- 2 zucchini or summer squash, cut into 1-inch pieces
- 1 teaspoon of dried thyme
- ½ teaspoon of dried oregano
- Freshly grated Parmesan cheese for serving, optional
- Crushed red pepper flakes, optional

Directions

1. Begin by preheating your oven to 425°.
2. Combine the veggies, garlic and the mushrooms in a large bowl and blend.
3. Drizzle with the olive oil.
4. Add the thyme, pepper, salt, and the dried oregano, then toss to allow it to combine.
5. Oil a baking pan to which take the potatoes and spread.
6. Roast the potatoes in the heated oven for about 10 minutes or so.
7. Remove the potatoes from the heat and introduce the mushrooms along with the vegetables.
8. Take it back to the oven for further roasting for 20 minutes.
9. Serve immediately with crushed pepper and sprinkle of grated parmesan.
10. Enjoy.

Pressure pot borscht

Ingredients

- 2 medium carrots (150 grams)
- 2 celery stalks (200 grams)
- 2 fresh beets (240 grams)
- 3 large potatoes (500 grams)
- 1 onion, medium-large
- 3 garlic cloves
- 4 tablespoons of sour cream
- 2 tablespoons of sunflower oil
- 1.5 cup of water (375 ml)
- 2 tablespoons of white wine vinegar
- 2 bay leaves
- 1 teaspoon of salt
- ¼ teaspoon of black pepper
- 4 cups of vegetable stock (1 liter)
- ¼ cup of tomato puree (50 grams)
- 9 ounces of white cabbage (300 grams)

Directions

1. Start by placing oil in to the inner pot of your Pressure pot.
2. Peel and dice the onion and place into the pot.

3. Press the sauté function and set to high.
4. Let sauté as you dice the veggies in stages and adding them to the pot.
5. Peel the carrots and cut into small pieces.
6. When ready, add them to the pot. Stir to mix.
7. Trim off the ends of celery then cut each stem in half lengthwise and dice into small pieces.
8. Add to the pot and stir to mix.
9. Remove the hard part from cabbage and cut.
10. Add to the pot and stir to mix.
11. Add the beets to the pot and stir again.
12. Add tomatoes into the pot, stir and turn off the sauté function.
13. Add the remaining ingredients apart from sour cream.
14. Lock the lid firmly in its position.
15. Turn the steam releasing valve to seal and press cooking.
16. Set the timer to 15 minutes and let it cook.
17. When ready, wait 10 minutes before releasing pressure manually.
18. Serve with a generous dollop of sour cream.
19. Enjoy.

Fresh huevos rancheros

Ingredients

For the Pico de Gallo

- ¼ cup of finely chopped white onion
- ¼ teaspoon of fine-grain sea salt
- 2 medium ripe tomatoes, chopped
- 2 tablespoons of lime juice
- ¼ cup of chopped fresh cilantro

For the refried beans

- Freshly ground black pepper, to taste
- ¼ teaspoon of fine-grain sea salt
- ½ teaspoon of lime juice
- 1 teaspoon of ground cumin
- 2 teaspoons of extra-virgin olive oil
- 1 can of black beans or pinto beans, rinsed and drained
- ¼ cup of water
- ¼ cup of finely chopped white onion

For Everything else

- ½ cup of shredded Monterey Jack cheese
- 1 ½ cups of your favorite red salsa
- Freshly ground black pepper

- 4 teaspoons of extra-virgin olive oil, divided
- 4 corn tortillas
- 4 eggs

Directions

1. In a medium bowl, combine the tomatoes together with the onion, cilantro, lime juice, and salt.
2. Stir to combine, set the bowl aside for later.
3. In a small saucepan over medium heat, warm the olive oil until shimmering but without smoke.
4. Add the onions and salt.
5. Let cook as you keep stirring occasionally, until the onions have softened in 6 minutes.
6. Then, add the cumin to the content let cook for 30 seconds as you keep stirring constantly, until fragrant.
7. Pour in the drained beans and water.
8. Stir, cover and let cook for 5 minutes.
9. Lower the heat, then remove the lid and mash up the beans about half of the beans.
10. Let continue to cook the beans when uncovered, stirring often for 3 minutes to thicken.
11. Then, remove the pot from the heat source and stir in the pepper and lime juice.
12. Taste and adjust accordingly.
13. Cover until you are ready to serve.

14. Pour the salsa into a medium saucepan over medium heat.
15. Bring the salsa to a simmer, stirring occasionally, and then reduce the heat let keep warm until serving.
16. In a small skillet over medium heat, warm each tortilla individually, flipping if needed.
17. Spread the black bean mixture over each tortilla and place each tortilla on an individual plate. Set aside.
18. In the same skillet over medium heat, pour in 1 teaspoon olive oil and wait until it's shimmering but not with smoke.
19. Break an egg and pour it into the skillet without breaking the yolk.
20. Fry the egg, lifting and tilting the pan occasionally to redistribute the oil, until the whites are set to the preferred level.
21. Place the fried egg on top of a prepared tortilla and repeat with the remaining eggs.
22. Spoon about ¼ of the warmed salsa across each dish, avoiding the egg yolk.
23. Use a slotted spoon to do the same with the Pico de Gallo, without the tomato juices.
24. Sprinkle with freshly ground black pepper and add any additional garnishes you might like.
25. Serve and enjoy immediately.

Chunky citrus avocado dip

The chunky citrus avocado borrowed the entire Mediterranean style that intrigues the taste buds leaving one to wanting more.

This is highly packed with flavors with a fine finishing.

Be sure to note that this dip has variations.

Ingredients

- ½ cup/ 60g chopped red onions
- Generous drizzle Early Harvest Greek extra virgin olive oil
- Juice of 1 lime
- 2 large avocados pitted, peeled and diced
- ½ cup chopped cilantro
- Salt and pepper
- ½ cup/ 7g of chopped fresh mint
- Cayenne
- ¾ tsp Sumac
- 1 ¾ or 49g crumbled feta cheese
- 2 Navel oranges, peeled and diced
- ½ cup/400g walnut hearts, chopped

Directions

1. Combine red onions, fresh herbs, avocado, oranges, and walnuts in a large bowl.
2. Season with pepper, salt, pinch of cayenne, and sumac.
3. Drizzle with early harvest extra virgin olive oil after adding lime juice.
4. Toss gently to blend and combine
5. Add the feta cheese on the top.
6. Serve and enjoy with chips of your choice.

Quick oven roasted tomatoes recipe

There are numerous ways of using the roasted tomatoes as a side dish typically in pasta or soup.

This can also be served with bruschetta style or on top of tossed bread.

Ingredients

- 2 or 3 minced garlic cloves
- Extra virgin olive oil
- 1 teaspoon of sumac
- 2 smaller tomatoes cut into halves
- Kosher salt and black pepper
- ½ teaspoon of dry chili pepper flakes
- 2 teaspoons of fresh thyme without stems
- Crumbled feta cheese, optional

Directions

1. Start by preheating your oven to 450°.
2. Place the tomatoes in a large bowl.
3. Add the minced garlic, pepper, salt, thyme and spices.

4. Drizzle with extra virgin olive oil, and toss to coat.

5. Transfer the tomatoes to a baking sheet that has a rim.

6. Spread the tomatoes in one layer with the flesh side facing up.

7. Put them in the heated oven for roasting for 30 – 35 minutes.

8. Remove off the heat source.

9. Garnish with fresh thyme and some sprinkles of feta cheese.

10. Serve while warm or at room temperature, depending to what you like.

Roasted cauliflower

This cauliflower recipe is a perfect make especially because of the possibility of combining it with various flavors.

Ingredients

- Handful fresh parsley for garnish optional
- 1 head cauliflower cored and divided into small florets
- ¼ cup/30 g toasted pine nuts or toasted slivered almonds, optional
- 2 teaspoons of ground cumin
- Salt and pepper
- Greek extra virgin olive oil
- 1 to 2 teaspoon of lemon juice or juice of ½ to 1 lemon to your liking
- 1 teaspoon of harissa spice

Directions

1. Preheat your oven to 250°.
2. Place the cauliflower florets on some large baking sheet.
3. To coat the florets, drizzle extra virgin olive oil and toss.
4. Add more extra virgin olive oil as needed.

5. Combine the harissa and cumin in a small sized dish, then season with the spice mixture and a pinch of black pepper and salt.
6. Re-toss to combine and bend
7. On the baking sheet evenly spread the cauliflower to form one layer.
8. Cover the baking sheet well with a foil and place at the center of preheated oven.
9. Roast while covered for 15 minutes.
10. Gently remove the foil with care, return the baking sheet to the oven.
11. Roast for another 20 – 30 minutes while you keep rotating the baking sheet and cauliflower with a pair of tongs.
12. If you intend to serve with tahini, now it is the time to make your tahini.
13. Remove the cauliflower from heat and transfer to a serving dish.
14. Immediately add lemon juice with some drizzle of tahini, parsley for garnish, and toasted nuts.
15. Sprinkle with harissa.
16. Serve with tahini as a sauce on the side
17. Enjoy.

Easy baked zucchini recipe with thyme and parmesan

With its golden crust, this golden zucchini is fantastic for a crowded pleaser served with some tzatziki sauce.

It should be served when still hot to enjoy the best out of it.

Ingredients

- ½ cup grated Parmesan cheese
- 1 teaspoon of dried oregano
- Extra virgin olive oil
- 3 to 4 zucchini trimmed and cut length-wise into quarters
- Pinch kosher salt
- ½ teaspoon of sweet paprika
- ½ teaspoon of black pepper
- 2 teaspoon of fresh thyme leaves no stems

Directions

1. Preheat the oven to about 350°
2. Mix together the grated Parmesan, thyme and spices until well combined in a small bowl at once.

3. Prepare a large baking sheet topped with a wire baking rack.
4. Lightly brush the baking rack with extra virgin olive oil.
5. Properly arrange the zucchini sticks with the skin side down right on the baking rack.
6. Brush every zucchini sticks with extra virgin olive oil
7. Sprinkle the Parmesan-thyme topping on each zucchini stick
8. Place in the preheated oven for 15 – 20 minutes.
9. Broil for 2 to 3 minutes while supervising closely.
10. Use tzatziki as an appetizer with a hummus for dipping.
11. Serve and enjoy.

Baba gaboughs recipe

This recipe utilizes the taste power in eggplants flavored with garlic, tahini, lime or lemon juice.

It is more delicious when served with homemade pita chips.

Ingredients

- Greek extra virgin olive oil
- 1 ½ tablespoon of tahini paste
- ½ teaspoon of sumac, more for garnish
- 1 tablespoon of lime or lemon juice, more if you like
- 1 large eggplant
- ½ teaspoon of cayenne pepper
- Parsley leaves for garnish
- 1 garlic clove
- Salt and pepper
- Toasted pine nuts for garnish
- 1 tablespoon of plain Greek yogurt (optional)

Directions

1. Begin by preheat your oven to 425°F.
2. Trim the top of the eggplant.

3. Using a knife, cut the eggplants in half then make a few slits in its skin.
4. Sprinkle the eggplant flesh then allow it to settle for few minutes and dab dry.
5. Place the eggplants cut in to halves in an upside down position placed on a baking sheet oiled with drizzle oil.
6. Bake in the preheated oven for 30 – 4- minutes until when the eggplants have totally softened.
7. Remove it off the heat sauce and let cool.
8. After cooling, scoop the flesh out and transfer to a colander and allow it to drain for up to 3 minutes.
9. Transfer eggplant to a bowl of a food processor attached with a blade.
10. Add tahini, lime juice, yogurt, pepper, salt, cayenne, and sumac.
11. Briefly run the food processor to blend the mixture.
12. In a small bowl, transfer and spread the baba ganoush.
13. Refrigerate while covered for 1 hour to allow the ganoush thicken a little.
14. Top the baba ganoush with a sprinkle of sumac right before serving with olive oil, parsley leaves, and toasted pine nuts.
15. Enjoy with warm pita bread.

Chicken sharwarma

This sharwarma recipe does not call for unique and special rotisseries to give it sweet delicious taste.

Baking it until tender with eastern spices is a perfect way served with pita pockets and other several Mediterranean salads as well as sauces.

Ingredients

- ¾ tablespoon of turmeric powder
- ¾ tablespoon of garlic powder
- ¾ tablespoon of ground coriander
- ¾ tablespoon of paprika
- Salt
- 1 large lemon juice
- ½ teaspoon of ground cloves
- ½ teaspoon of cayenne pepper
- 1/3 cup of extra virgin olive oil
- 1 large thinly sliced onions
- 8 boneless and skinless chicken thighs
- ¾ tablespoon of ground cumin
- 6 pita pockets
- Baby arugula
- Pickles or Kalamata olives

- Tahini sauce
- 3-ingredient Mediterranean salad

Directions

1. In a small bowl, mix majority of the ingredients typically the coriander, turmeric, cumin, garlic power, paprika, and cloves.
2. Keep the sharwarma spice for later
3. Pat the chicken thighs dry and season with salt on both sides.
4. Then thinly slice into small bite-sized pieces.
5. Put the chicken in a large bowl to Add the shawarma spices, then toss to coat.
6. Introduce the onions, olive oil, and lemon juice.
7. Toss everything together again.
8. Cover totally for refrigeration for up to 3 hours. If there is time for you to wait, refrigerate overnight.
9. Preheat your oven to 425 - 430°.
10. Transfer the chicken from the fridge to outside and allow it to heat to room temperature for some minutes.
11. Spread the marinated chicken with the onions in one layer on a large lightly-oiled baking sheet pan.
12. Start to roast in the heated oven for 30 minutes.

13. To obtain a proper brown crispy chicken, you can move the pan closer to heat source and briefly while supervising closely.
14. As the chicken is still roasting, keep preparing the pitas pockets, make the tahini sauce, tzatziki sauce and the 3-ingredient Mediterranean salad to set side.
15. Serve in the pitas by spreading a little tahini sauce or tzatziki sauce.
16. Add the chicken shawarma, Mediterranean salad, arugula, and pickles or olives
17. Serve immediately and enjoy

Crispy homemade fish sticks

These fish sticks are prepared to be totally tender on the inside and completely crispy on the outside.

The seasoning gives it the flavor that anyone is seeking for in any dish or meal.

A salmon or white firm fish is just fantastic to make the best of this recipe.

Ingredients

- Parsley garnish
- Salt
- Zest of 1 lemon juice
- ½ of lemon juice for finishing
- ½ cup of bread crumbs
- 1 cup of parmesan
- Extra virgin olive oil
- 1 teaspoon of pepper
- 1 teaspoon of sweet paprika
- 1 teaspoon of totally dried oregano
- 1 ½ lb. of firm fish fillet skinless
- ½ cup of flour
- 1 egg beaten in 1 tablespoon of water

- Tahini sauce

Directions

1. Heat your oven to 450°.
2. Pat the fish fillet dry and season with kosher salt on either sides.
3. Cut the fish fillet into pieces
4. Combine the dried oregano, paprika, and the black pepper in a small bowl.
5. Season the cut fish fillets on every side with the spice mixture.
6. Ensure to make a dredging station, then in a small shallow dish place the flour.
7. In a deeper bowl, place the egg wash next to the flour dish. Get a separate dish for combing grated parmesan, bread crumbs, and lemon zest, and place adjacent to the bowl containing the egg wash.
8. Coat the fish by dipping them in the flour, shake of the excess flour.
9. Deep the fish in the bowl of egg wash.
10. From the egg wash bowl, dip it again in the bread crumbs and parmesan mixture.
11. Repeat the process until all the fish sticks are coated.

12. On an oiled baking sheet, arrange the coated fish, brush extra virgin olive oil. Place the baking sheet in the middle of the already heated oven and bake for 12 - -15 minutes.

13. Finish with lemon zest and fresh lemon juice. Garnish with parsley.

14. Choose your favorite sauce to serve with either tahini or tzatziki with salad typically Mediterranean white beans salad.

15. Enjoy

Falafel recipe

Ingredients

- 7-8 garlic cloves, peeled
- 1 cup fresh parsley leaves, stems removed
- 1 tablespoon of ground cumin
- 1 tablespoon of ground coriander
- 1 teaspoon of cayenne pepper, optional
- Oil for frying
- 1 tablespoon of ground black pepper
- ¾ cup fresh cilantro leaves, stems removed
- 2 tablespoon of toasted sesame seeds
- ½ teaspoon of baking soda
- 1 small onion, quartered
- 2 cups dried chickpeas
- ½ cup fresh dill, stems removed
- Baby Arugula
- Tomatoes, chopped or diced
- Tahini Sauce
- Salt to taste
- Cucumbers, chopped or diced
- 1 teaspoon of baking powder
- Pita pockets
- Pickles

Directions

1. 24 hours prior to cooking, place the baking soda and the dried chickpeas in a bowl of water covering the chickpeas by 2 inches.
2. Drain the chickpeas when completely soaked, pat dry.
3. Add the chickpeas, herbs, onions, garlic and spices to a food processor fitted with a blade.
4. Run the food processor for about 40 seconds at a time until all is well combined to form the falafel mixture.
5. Change the falafel mixture to a container, then cover tightly for refrigeration for about 1 hour.
6. Add the baking powder and sesame seeds right before frying the mixture and stir using a spoon.
7. Make patties out of the falafel mixture ½ inch thick.
8. Put oil in a medium sized saucepan and heat with a medium temperature to form soft bubbles.
9. Place the falafel patties in the oil fry for 3 – 5 minutes until medium brown on the outside.
10. In a plate lined with paper, place the falafel to drain the oil.
11. While hot, serve the falafel on small plates with pita bread, tomatoes, cucumber or tahini.

Greek-style black eyed peas

The green style black eyed peas are a wonderful recipe to feed a crowd on a limited budget yet healthy and hearty.

Onions and garlic with Greek spices give it a flavorful taste when finished with citrus.

Ingredients

- 2 15 ounces cans of black eyed peas, rinsed and drained
- 1 lime or lemon juice
- 1 chopped green bell pepper
- Kosher salt and black pepper
- 1 large chopped yellow onion
- 1 teaspoon of dry oregano
- 1 cup chopped fresh parsley
- 4 chopped garlic cloves
- ½ teaspoon of paprika
- Extra virgin olive oil
- 1 15 ounces of can diced tomato
- 2 cups water
- 1 dry bay leaf
- 2 - 3 carrots, peeled and chopped
- 1 ½ teaspoon of ground cumin

- ½ teaspoon of red pepper flakes, optional

Directions

1. In a large pot, heat extra virgin olive oil over medium temperature until shimmering
2. Add onions and garlic to Sauté shortly until fragrant and translucent.
3. Add bell peppers and carrots and cook for 5 minutes while tossing frequently.
4. Add juicy diced tomatoes. Bay leaf, water, salt, spices, and pepper.
5. Increase the temperature and let boil.
6. Introduce the black eyed peas and boil for 5 minutes after which reduce the heat.
7. Cover half-way and let simmer for 25 – 30 minutes.
8. Add little water if the stew is too dry
9. Stir in the parsley and lemon juice.
10. Change to bowels and drizzle with extra virgin olive oil and serve.
11. Enjoy with your best grains or warm Greek pita.

Mediterranean-style Juicy salmon burgers

Tired or do not like dry burgers?

Enjoy this juicy salmon burger spiced with lemon juice and served with tomatoes and arugula.

Ingredients

- 1 red onion, sliced
- 1 ½ lb. skinless salmon fillet, cut into chunks
- 1 teaspoon of ground sumac
- Bread of your choice (optional)
- ½ teaspoon of black pepper
- 6 baby arugula
- Kosher Salt
- ½ teaspoon of sweet paprika
- Italian bread crumbs for coating
- ¼ cup extra virgin olive oil
- 1 lemon
- 1 cup chopped fresh parsley
- 2-3 tablespoon minced green onions
- Homemade Tzatziki Sauce
- 2 teaspoon of Dijon mustard

- 1 tomato, sliced into rounds
- 1 teaspoon of ground coriander

Directions

1. Put ¼ of the salmon in a bowl of a large food processor together with mustard Dijon then run processor to form a pasty mixture
2. Move to a bowl.
3. Put the remaining salmon in the food processor, and pulse a few times until coarsely chopped into ¼-inch pieces
4. Move to the same bowl.
5. Add minced green parsley, onions, coriander, paprika, sumac, and black pepper.
6. Season with kosher salt, then blend properly until the mixture is totally combined.
7. Cover to refrigerate for 30 hours.
8. While the salmon chills, prepare the toppings.
9. Make the Greek Tzatziki Sauce.
10. Prepare the sliced tomatoes, arugula, and the remaining toppings and buns to serve.
11. When all these above three parts are ready, bring the salmon out of the fridge.
12. Divide into 4 equal parts and form into 1-inch think patties.

13. Put bread crumbs on a plate.
14. Put each patty in the bread crumbs plate, then coat on both sides.
15. Move the breaded salmon patties on a sheet pan lined with parchment paper.
16. Cook salmon patties.
17. Heat 3 tablespoons of extra virgin olive oil over medium temperature until shimmering without smoke.
18. Bring down the salmon patties gently continue to cook for 2 – 4 minutes while turning over once until when lightly brown on all sides. Regulate the temperature as necessary.
19. Arrange cooked salmon burgers onto paper towel to drain any excess oil
20. Sprinkle lightly if you desire with Kosher salt.
21. Squeeze of fresh lemon juice on top.
22. Assemble in prepared buns.
23. Spread the buns with a bit of tzatziki sauce.
24. Add the salmon, then layer on the arugula, onion slices, and tomato
25. Serve and enjoy

Greek-style eggplant recipe

Greek-style eggplant recipe is a total meatless velvet prepared with chickpeas and tomatoes. It can serve as dinner or just side dish with the delicious satisfaction that everyone is seeking for.

Ingredients

- 1.5 lb. eggplant, cut into cubes
- 1 teaspoon of organic ground coriander
- Fresh herbs such as parsley and mint for garnish
- 1 28 ounces can of chopped tomato
- 2 15 ounces cans chickpeas, reserve the canning liquid
- 6 large garlic cloves, minced
- ½ teaspoon of black pepper
- 2 dry bay leaves
- Kosher salt
- 1 large yellow onion, chopped
- 1 green bell pepper, stem and innards removed and diced
- ½ teaspoon of organic ground turmeric
- Extra Virgin Olive Oil
- 1 carrot, chopped
- 1 to 1 ½ tsp sweet paprika OR smoked paprika
- ¾ teaspoon of ground cinnamon

- 1 teaspoon of dry oregano

Directions

1. Preheat the oven to 400°.
2. Put cut eggplant cubes in a colander over a large bowl to sprinkle with salt.
3. Keep aside for 20 minutes to give room for the eggplant to "sweat out" any bitterness.
4. Rinse with water, then pat dry.
5. Heat ¼ cup of extra virgin olive oil over medium to shimmer.
6. Add peppers, onions, and chopped carrot allow to cook for 2 – 3 minutes while constantly stirring.
7. Add garlic, spices, bay leaf, and a dash of salt.
8. Let cook for another minute keeping stirring until fragrant.
9. Add the chickpeas, eggplant, chopped tomato, reserved chickpea liquid and stir to blend.
10. Cook at a rolling point for 10 minutes.
11. Remove from stove top, cover and move to oven.
12. Continue to cook in oven for 45 minutes until eggplant is totally cooked.
13. Remove from oven when ready
14. Add a drizzle of extra virgin olive oil, parsley or mint.
15. Serve hot with side Greek yogurt, pita bread or tzatziki sauce.

Easy Moroccan vegetable tagine

This is a simple vegan packed vegetable stew with several Moroccan flavors.

It is entirely gluten free; thus healthy.

Ingredients

- 1 teaspoon of ground coriander
- 1-quart low-sodium vegetable broth
- 2 large carrots, peeled and chopped
- 2 large russet potatoes, peeled and cubed
- ½ cup heaping chopped dried apricot
- 1 large sweet potato, peeled and cubed
- Salt
- ¼ cup extra virgin olive oil, more for later
- 2 medium yellow onions, peeled and chopped
- Handful fresh parsley leaves
- • 1 tablespoon Harissa spice blend
- 8 – 10 garlic cloves, peeled and chopped
- 1 teaspoon of ground cinnamon
- 1 lemon, juice of
- 2 cups canned whole peeled tomatoes
- ½ teaspoon of ground turmeric
- 2 cups cooked chickpeas

Directions

1. In a heavy large pot, heat olive oil over medium heat until shimmering.
2. Add onions and increase the temperature to medium-high.
3. Sauté for 5 minutes while tossing frequently.
4. Add garlic and all chopped veggies to the solution, then Season with salt and spices, then toss again to combine.
5. Cook for about 5 – 7 minutes on medium-high temperature stirring regularly.
6. Add apricot, tomatoes, and broth. Season with a small dash of salt.
7. Keep the heat on medium allow to cook for 10 minutes.
8. Lower the heat, cover properly and let simmer for 20 – 25 minutes until veggies are tender.
9. Stir in chickpeas cook for 5 minutes on low heat.
10. Introduce the lemon juice and fresh parsley while stirring.
11. Taste and adjust seasoning.
12. Transfer to serving bowls and top each with a generous drizzle of extra virgin olive oil.
13. Serve hot with rice, bread or couscous.

Simple Mediterranean olive pasta

The Mediterranean olive pasta is fully loaded with Mediterranean Sea diet flavors.

It derives its sweet taste from this flavors.

Ingredients

- Zest of 1 lemon
- 6 ounces of marinated artichoke hearts, drained
- 1 lb. thin spaghetti
- ¼ cup pitted olives, halved
- ¼ cup crumbled feta cheese, more if you like
- 12 ounces of grape tomatoes, halved
- 1 cup chopped fresh parsley
- 1 teaspoon black pepper
- ½ cup early harvest Greek extra virgin olive oil
- Salt
- 10-15 fresh basil leaves, torn
- 4 garlic cloves, crushed
- 3 scallions of green onions, top trimmed, all whites and greens chopped
- Crushed red pepper flakes (optional)

Directions

1. Cook thin spaghetti pasta to al dente according to package instruction.
2. Heat the extra virgin olive oil in a large cast iron skillet over medium heat When pasta is almost cooked.
3. Reduce the heat immediately add garlic and a pinch of salt.
4. Cook briefly for 10 seconds keep stirring regularly.
5. Stir in the parsley, chopped scallions, and tomatoes.
6. Over low heat, Cook until just warmed through for 30 seconds.
7. Remove from heat, when ready and drain off extra cooking water.
8. Return to the cooking pot.
9. Add the warmed olive oil sauce in toss to coat.
10. Toss again to coat after adding black pepper.
11. Add all the remaining ingredients and toss.
12. Immediately serve in pasta bowls.
13. Top each with more basil leaves and feta
14. Enjoy!

Mediterranean roasted vegetable barley

This utilizes the sweetness magic in fresh herbs, citrus and extra virgin olive oil to trick one's taste buds.

Ingredients

- Water
- 2 whole zucchini squash and diced
- Early Harvest Greek extra virgin olive oil
- 1 garlic clove, minced
- 1 163 g dry pearl barley, washed
- 2 scallions of green onions, trimmed and chopped
- 1 medium red onion and diced
- 1 yellow bell pepper, cored and diced
- 1 red bell pepper, cored and diced
- salt and pepper
- 2 teaspoon of harissa spice , divided
- ¾ teaspoon of smoked paprika , divided
- 2 tablespoon of fresh squeezed lemon juice
- 56 g chopped fresh parsley
- Toasted pine nuts (optional)
- Feta cheese

Instruction

1. Preheat your oven to 425°.
2. In a saucepan, put pearl barley and 2 ½ cups water.
3. Boil, then reduce the heat to low.
4. Cover and cook for 40 – 45 minutes.
5. As the barley cooks, add all diced vegetables on a large baking sheet.
6. Season with salt, pepper, 1 ½ teaspoon of harissa spice, and ½ teaspoon of smoked paprika.
7. Drizzle with extra virgin olive oil and toss to coat.
8. Spread evenly in one layer on the baking sheet.
9. Roast in the heated oven for 25 minutes.
10. Drain the excess water when barley is ready.
11. Season again with salt, pepper, ½ teaspoon of harissa spice and ¼ teaspoon of smoked paprika toss again to make sure it combines.
12. Move the barley to a large mixing bowl.
13. Add roasted veggies.
14. Add chopped garlic, scallions, and fresh parsley.
15. Dress with lemon juice
16. Drizzle with Early Harvest extra virgin olive oil and Toss.
17. If desired, top with toasted pine nuts and crumbled feta.
18. Serve warm, cold or at room temperature.
19. Enjoy

Couscous recipe

In only 15 minutes, you can make couscous recipe with handful ingredients. Couscous serves as the best side next to your favorite protein or exciting bed to a tasty stew as desired.

Ingredients

- 1 cup dry instant couscous
- 1 cup low-sodium broth or water
- Extra virgin olive oil
- Kosher Salt
- Fresh herbs to your liking, optional
- Pinch of cumin optional
- 2 green onions, chopped, optional
- 1 – 2 garlic clove, minced, Sautéed in an extra virgin olive oil, optional

Directions

1. Add broth or water in a saucepan.
2. Add a drizzle of extra virgin olive oil together with a pinch of kosher salt.
3. Bring to a boil.
4. Toast the couscous.

5. Heat 1 – 2 tablespoon of extra virgin olive oil.

6. Add the couscous and toss around with a wooden spoon for it to turn golden brown to add desired flavor. Optional

7. Stir in the couscous quickly and turn the heat off soon enough.

8. Cover and let settle for 10 minutes for the couscous to absorbed all the water.

9. Uncover and fluff with a fork.

10. Serve couscous plain.

11. To flavor it up mix in spices and herbs.

12. If desired, add in a pinch of cumin, chopped green onions, Sautéed garlic, and fresh herbs

13. Enjoy.

Mediterranean-style tuna pasta

20 minutes is just sufficient to make this darn delicious tuna pasta with highly bold flavors.

The ingredients are quite simple ingredients typically parsley, lemon zest parmesan and others listed below.

Ingredients

- ½ lemon juice
- 1 ½ cups frozen peas
- 1 red bell pepper, cored and cut into thin strips
- Black pepper
- 6 garlic cloves, minced
- 6 – 8 pitted Kalamata olives sliced
- Extra virgin olive oil
- Zest of 1 lemon
- ¾ lb. spaghetti
- Handful chopped fresh parsley
- 1 tsp dried oregano
- 2 – 5 ounces of cans solid albacore tuna, drained
- Grated Parmesan cheese
- Kosher salt
- 1 sliced jalapeno pepper (optional)

Directions

1. Boil 3 quarts of water to a rolling boil with 1 tablespoon of kosher salt.

2. Cook the pasta in the boiling water as per the package Directions

3. Add the frozen peas to the cooked pasta continue to cook for the remaining time about 2 – 4 minutes.

4. Take ¾ cup of the cooking water and set it aside after the pasta is ready.

5. Drain the water in the pasta and peas in a colander.

6. In a deep large cooking pan, heat 2 tablespoons of extra virgin olive oil over medium temperature to shimmering without smoke.

7. Introduce the red bell peppers

8. Cook for 3 – 4 minutes while tossing frequently.

9. Add the garlic cook and toss again frequently for 30 seconds until fragrant.

10. It is the right time to add the cooked pasta and peas to the pan and toss to combine.

11. Add the lemon zest, jalapeno, tuna, parsley, lemon juice, oregano, black pepper, Kalamata olives, and heavy sprinkle of Parmesan cheese.

12. Drizzle a small extra virgin olive oil and pasta cooking water as necessary.

13. Toss everything.

14. Taste and adjust seasoning accordingly

15. Serve the pasta and enjoy.

Greek lemon rice

Onions, lemon juice, garlic, and fresh herbs give this meal a wonderful flavor.

These flavors have made Greek lemon rice a favorite dinner meal for many individuals and families.

Ingredients

- Early Harvest Greek extra virgin olive oil
- Pinch salt
- 1 garlic clove, minced
- 1 teaspoon of dry dill weed
- 1 zest of lemon
- 2 lemons
- Large handful chopped fresh parsley
- 2 cups of raw long grain rice
- ½ cup orzo pasta
- 1 medium yellow onion, chopped
- 2 cups low sodium broth

Directions

1. Thoroughly wash the rice, then soak it for approximately 15 – 20 minutes in cold water sufficient enough to fully immerse the rice at least by 1 inch.

2. Drain out all the water

3. In a large sauce pan with a lid, heat 3 tablespoons of extra virgin olive oil to shimmer without smoke.

4. Add onions and cook for 3 – 4 minutes until when it becomes translucent.

5. Then add the garlic together with the orzo pasta.

6. Toss shortly to give the orzo some color then stir in the rice continue to toss to coat.

7. Introduce the broth and lemon juice let the liquid to boil at a rolling boil point.

8. Lower the heat, keep rice covered and cook for about 20 minutes.

9. Remove rice from heat.

10. Let it simmer for about 10 minutes for better outcome and taste.

11. Uncover and stir in dill weed, parsley, and lemon zest.

12. Garnish with lemon on top.

13. Enjoy.

Mediterranean sole

The Mediterranean sole is famous because of its incredible sweet aroma flavor steamed in a parchment.

This recipe cannot be left out when one is looking for a healthy fish and vegetable meal.

It should be noted that white fish is the best option if a person decides not to use the sole.

Fins the simplest recipe shown below.

Ingredients

- 1 pound of sole fillets divided into four equal portions
- A quarter spoonful of pepper
- Dried white wine or chicken broth measured in two tablespoons
- One medium lemon, properly sliced
- Half cup of Greek olives
- Two cups of cherry tomatoes in halves
- One tablespoon of fresh lemon juice
- One spoonful capers, should be drained
- Garlic cloves minced
- Two tablespoon of freshly minced parsley

Cooking Directions

1. Heat the oven to 400°, then place every fillet on a piece of a heavy foil which is 12 in. square. Evenly sprinkle the fillets with the pepper. Follow by toping with lemon slices. Drizzle with wine and 1 table spoon of olive oil.

2. Mixed tomatoes, capers, olives, lemon juice, garlic and 1more tablespoon of oil spread over the fillets. Fold the foil around all the fish. Then seal it so tightly.

3. Place all the packets on your baking sheet. Continue baking until the fish starts to easily flake when tapped with a fork for 10 to 12 minutes. Allow the steam to escape by unsealing the packets carefully. Spread the top with parsley.

4. Serve your Mediterranean sole and enjoy.

Juicy and delicious mixed spice burgers

This recipe is for a street food.

Nevertheless, it can be prepared at home for dishes especially gyros and the spiced burgers referred to as kofta.

Well, the recipe for making a quick juicy and delicious mixed spiced burger is below right here.

Ingredients

- 1 medium sized finely chopped onions
- ½ teaspoon of ground cinnamon
- 1 minced garlic glove
- ¾ teaspoon of ground allspice
- ¾ teaspoon pepper
- 2 teaspoons of freshly minced mint
- 3 tablespoons of minced parsley
- ½ teaspoon of salt
- Lettuce leaves and refrigerated tzatziki sauce
- 1 pounds of lean ground beef
- ¼ teaspoon ground nutmeg

Instruction

1. Combine all the ingredients in a large bowl except lean ground beef and lettuce leaves.
2. Then, add the lean beef mix thoroughly.
3. Shape it into 6 4*2-in oblong patties
4. Grill the patties fully covered in a medium heat for not more than 6 minute on every side. The heat should rise up to 160°.
5. Place the lettuce leaves
6. Serve with sauce

Mediterranean cauliflower

This cauliflower dish is prepared easily with a handful of ingredients with a skillet.

Therefore, this takes the cauliflower to a whole new taste horizon from the ordinary less-taste cauliflower dish.

Find the step-by-step cooking Directions below.

Ingredients

- 1 large head of cauliflower
- 2 cans of diced tomatoes with basil, garlic, and oregano drained
- 4 green sliced onions
- ¼ teaspoon of salt
- ½ cups of sliced olives with pimientos
- 1 cup crumbled feta cheese
- ½ teaspoon of pepper

Directions

1. Using a stockpot about 6-qt, put a steamer basket over 1 in. of fresh water.
2. Careful place the cauliflower in the basket.

3. Bring it to a boil reduce the heat

4. Cover the steam until crisp tender in about 4 – 6minutes.

5. Drain all the water and return it to the pan.

6. Place and stir in the onions, olives, tomatoes, pepper and salt.

7. Return to boil again

8. Reduce the heat, simmer carefully.

9. Uncover the cauliflower until it is just tender; heat the tomatoes through for 3 – 5 minutes.

10. Sprinkle with feta cheese and serve your dish and enjoy

Garlic asiago cauliflower rice

This is a 5 ingredient low carb side dish. The seasoning of garlic and asiago means a pack of punch to the tommy.

The ingredients and Directions are detailed below.

Ingredients

- 1 medium size head cauliflower
- ½ cups of finely grated asiago cheese
- 1 tablespoon of extra virgin olive oil
- 2 tablespoons of unsalted butter
- ½ teaspoon of garlic herb seasoning blend

Directions

1. In a food processor firmly fitted with a steel blade, shed the cauliflower which should measure 6 cups.
2. In a heavy skillet or cast-iron, combine and heat the butter and oil and blend over a medium to high heat.
3. Immediately after the butter melts, gently stir in the cauliflower
4. Cook without covering for about 10 – 15 minutes until tender
5. Occasionally stir (use about 4 cups of cauliflower rice)

6. Add cheese and stir until when well combined.

7. Serve

Greek brown and wild rice bowls

The Greek brown and wild rice is a short ingredient recipe stuffed with much flavor.

If you go for a hand-held version, you can leave the rice and tuck the all the ingredients in a pita pocket.

The ingredients and instruction are right here below.

Ingredients

- 1 pack of ready to serve whole grain brown and wild rice (should weigh 8 – ½ ounces)
- Minced fresh parsley
- ¼ cup of crumbled feta cheese
- ¼ cup of Greek vinaigrette
- ½ medium ripe avocado sliced
- ¾ cup of cherry tomatoes divided into halves
- ¼ cup of pitted Greek olives slices

Directions

1. Using a microwave with a safe bowl, mix the rice with 2 tablespoons of vinaigrette.

2. Cover completely and cook a high temperature for about 2 minutes.

3. Separate between 2 bowls.

4. Top with avocado, cheese, olives, tomatoes, and add parsley if desired.

5. Serve

Tips

To increase the protein content, one can add tuna or grilled chicken to the bowls

Lemony chickpeas

These chickpeas are suitable over fluffy brown rice to boost a meatless meal which you will definitely love.

Check the ingredients and Directions below.

Ingredients

- 2 cups of uncooked instant brown rice
- 3 tablespoons lemon juice
- ½ teaspoon of grated lemon zest
- 1 cup of vegetable broth
- ¼ teaspoon crushed red pepper flakes
- 1 can of diced undrained tomatoes
- 2 cans of rinsed and drained chickpeas
- 1 tablespoon of olive oil
- 1 medium chopped onions
- ¼ teaspoon of pepper

Directions

1. Cook your rice normally
2. Using a large skillet, heat oil with a medium heat.
3. Add the onions

4. Cook for about 3 – 4 minutes while occasionally stirring until tender
5. Introduce the chickpeas, broth, pepper flakes, tomatoes and bring to boil
6. Reduce the heat, simmer and keep covered for 10 minutes to give room for flavors to blend in.
7. Uncover and allow to simmer for 4 – 5 minutes until when the water inside reduces slightly; keep stirring occasionally.
8. Add the lemon juice and lemon zest.
9. Serve with rice

Tahini dressing

Tahini dressing is best to serve with salad of romaine lettuce, baby red potatoes, asparagus and snap peas.

This presents a healthy style of starting a meal.

Tahini tastes like a sweet peanuts butter of course with a shaper flavor and aroma of a puree of pure sesame.

The recipe cook direction is as below beginning with the ingredients.

Ingredients

- ½ cup water
- 3 tablespoons lemon juice
- 4 garlic cloves
- ½ cup tahini
- 1/8 teaspoon pepper
- ¼ teaspoon salt
- 1 teaspoon ground cumin
- ¼ teaspoon cayenne pepper

Directions

1. Introduce all ingredients in a blender at the same time.
2. Cover and blend until ready
3. Serve

Moroccan chickpeas stew

Ingredients

- 2 cups cubed peeled butternut squash; ½-inch cubes
- 1 tablespoon olive oil
- 1 can (14-½ ounces) diced tomatoes, undrained
- ¼ teaspoon ground cumin
- 1 teaspoon ground cinnamon
- 1 can (15 ounces) chickpeas or garbanzo beans, rinsed and drained
- ½ teaspoon pepper
- ¼ teaspoon ground ginger
- Chopped cilantro (optional)
- 1 large onion, chopped
- ¼ teaspoon salt
- 1 large sweet red pepper, chopped
- 1 cup water

Directions

1. Using an oven preferably Dutch oven, begin by heating the oil with a medium to high temperature.
2. Add onions, red pepper, and squash.

3. Cook while stirring until when the onions become translucent and the red pepper becomes crispy tender in about 5 minutes.
4. Stir in seasonings until fully blended
5. Introduce chickpeas, tomatoes, and water.
6. Bring the combination to boil
7. Reduce the heat, simmer and cover for about 8 minutes until squash is tender
8. If desired, you can top with cilantro
9. Serve

Tips

One can add color with an extra layer of flavor and aroma with a chopped cilantro garnish.

Lemon chicken skewers

This lemon chicken skewers recipe has always been a famous option at hit parties.

The recipe includes a tender chunk of chicken and fresh from garden vegetables.

Below is the recipe ingredients and Directions.

Ingredients

- ¼ teaspoon dried oregano
- 3 tablespoons lemon juice
- ¼ cup olive oil
- 1-½ pounds boneless skinless chicken breasts, cut into 1-½-in. pieces
- 2 garlic cloves, minced
- 12 cherry tomatoes
- 1 tablespoon white wine vinegar
- 3 medium onions, cut into wedges
- 3 medium zucchini, halved lengthwise and cut into 1-½-inch slices
- 1 teaspoon salt
- ¼ teaspoon pepper
- ½ teaspoon sugar
- 2 teaspoons grated lemon zest

Directions

1. Combine nine ingredients except the boneless skinless chicken breasts, zucchini, onions and tomatoes in a large bowl.
2. Set aside about ¼ cup for basting.
3. Pour the combined ingredients in the large bowl.
4. Introduce in the chicken and turn to coat.
5. Pour the marinade balance into separate large bowl
6. Add the zucchini, tomatoes, and onions then turn to coat.
7. Full cover and refrigerate the chicken and the veggies for a whole 4 hours. One can also refrigerate overnight; it is okay.
8. Carefully drain and through away the marinade
9. Serve and enjoy your healthy meal

Feta frittata

Are you having a lazy Sunday?

If yes, then this is the perfect recipe for you to enjoy your Sunday.

The chopped tomatoes and feta cheese are the special ingredients that make this frittata unique tossed with salad for a perfect light healthy Mediterranean lunch.

Ingredients

- 1 small minced garlic glove
- 2 large eggs
- 1 small thinly sliced green onion
- 4 tablespoons of crumbled feta cheese which must be divided
- 1/3 cup of chopped plum tomato
- ½ cup egg substitute
- 2 tablespoons of reduced fat sour cream
- 4 thin slices of peeled avocado

Directions

1. Start by heating oil 6-in. nonstick skillet over medium temperature.
2. Then Sauté garlic and onion until when tender.
3. Whisk both eggs (egg and egg substitute) and 3 tablespoons of feta cheese.
4. Introduce the mixture to the skillet (note; this mixture must immediately settle to the edges).
5. Properly cover and set to cook for 4 – 6 minutes.
6. Sprinkle the remaining 1 tablespoon of feta cheese and tomatoes.
7. Cover again and cook until the eggs are completely set for another 2 – 3 minutes.
8. Leave it to for 5 minutes.
9. Cut in half and serve with the sour cream and avocado
10. Enjoy

Zucchini and cheese roulades

Ingredients

- 4 medium zucchini
- 1/8 teaspoon of salt
- 1 cup of part-skim ricotta cheese
- 1/8 teaspoon of pepper
- 1 tablespoon of lemon juice
- 1 tablespoon of chopped Greek olives
- ¼ cup of grated parmesan cheese
- 1 tablespoon of drained capers
- 2 tablespoon of minced basil (dry of fresh basil)

Directions

1. Use a small bowl to mix all the nine ingredients except zucchini
2. Slice the zucchini lengthwise to make 24 1/8-in slices which must be thick
3. On a properly greased grill rack, separate the zucchini in batches and cook while covered over a medium temperature
4. Continue to grill for 2 – 3 minutes on each side until tender.

5. On the end of each zucchini slice, put 1 tablespoon of the ricotta mixture.

6. Roll each of them up and lock with a toothpick

7. Enjoy

Quinoa with peas and onions

This dish is a real source of proteins; which picky eaters may find loving.

It is ideal to use frozen peas instead of shelled ones.

Below are the ingredients and directions for the preparation.

Ingredients

- 2 tablespoons of chopped walnuts
- ¼ teaspoons of pepper
- ½ teaspoons of salt
- 1 tablespoon of olive oil
- 1 – ½ cups of frozen peas
- 1 small chopped onions
- 2 cups of water
- 1 cup of rinsed quinoa

Directions

1. Using a large saucepan, boil water.
2. Add quinoa to the water.
3. Reduce the heat and cover to simmer for 12 – 15 minutes and or until the water it absorbed.

4. Take it off the heat source and fluff with a fork.
5. In a large skillet, Sauté onions in oil until when they are tender.
6. Introduce the peas
7. Cook and stir until it is heated through.
8. Gently stir in the cooked quinoa, pepper and the salt.
9. Sprinkle evenly with the walnuts
10. Serve

Mediterranean tilapia

The taste of tilapia is quite mild which is easy to spice with ingredients. Furthermore, fish has low calorie and fat content making it a perfect Mediterranean Sea diet.

Below are the ingredients and step by step instruction.

Ingredients

- ½ cup of crumbled feta cheese
- 1 cup of canned diced tomatoes
- ½ cup of water packed artichoke chopped hearts
- ½ cup of ripe slices of olives
- 6 tilapia fillets weighing about 6 ounces each

Directions

1. Start by preheating the oven up to 400°.
2. Put the fillets in a baking pan highly coated with cooking spray
3. Top with artichokes hearts, olives, cheese and tomatoes.
4. While uncovered, bake until the fish can flake easily when turned with a fork, in 15 – 20 minutes.
5. The meal is ready for serving

Mediterranean spinach and beans

Ingredients

- 6 ounces of fresh baby spinach; eight cups
- ¼ teaspoon of salt
- 1 can of water packed artichoke hearts (should be rinsed and thoroughly drained)
- ¼ teaspoon of pepper
- 1 can of cannellini beans washed and drained
- 1/8 teaspoon of crushed red pepper flakes
- 1 tablespoon of olive oil
- 2 minced garlic cloves
- 1 can of no salt added diced tomatoes undrained
- 2 teaspoon of Worcestershire sauce
- 1 small chopped onions

Directions

1. Using a 12-in skillet, heat oil over medium temperature
2. Sauté the onions for 3 – 5 minutes until they are tender
3. Introduce garlic
4. Cook and stir for about 1 minute

5. Introduce the tomatoes and Worcestershire including the seasonings and boil.
6. Reduce the heat and allow to simmer when uncovered to evaporate the liquid for 6 – 8 minutes
7. Introduce the beans, spinach and artichokes hearts
8. Place it for cooking until the spinach is visibly wilted in 3 – 5 minutes
9. You can drizzle with additional oil and serve

Mediterranean stuffed chicken breast

Ingredients

- 1 teaspoon of Greek seasoning
- 4 boneless skinless chicken breasts divided into half weighing 6 ounces each
- 1 cup of crumbled feta cheese.
- 1/3 cup of chopped oil packed sundried tomatoes
- 2 tablespoons of olive oil from sundried tomatoes

Directions

1. Preheat the open up to 375°.
2. Mix the cheese and tomatoes in a small bowl
3. Using a meat mallet, pound the chicken breast to ¼-in thick.
4. Evenly brush with 1 teaspoon of oil.
5. Sprinkle with Greek seasoning.
6. Top with a mixture of cheese.
7. Roll the chicken breasts form the shorter side; lock with a toothpick.
8. Put it in a 11*7-in. baking dish, seam side down and brush with the oil balance.

9. Bake while uncovered for 30 – 35 minutes. Or wait until the thermometer reads 165°.

10. Remove and discard the toothpicks

11. Serve

Mediterranean broccoli and cheese omelet

This recipe works for breakfast, lunch, and dinner.

It can also be served on Italian bread. Furthermore, this recipe is suitable for utilizing a broccoli left over.

The following are the ingredients and step-by-step Directions.

Ingredients

- Shaved Romano cheese and minced parsley
- 1 tablespoon of olive oil
- ¼ teaspoon of pepper
- 1/3 cup of grated Romano cheese
- ½ teaspoon of salt
- 1/3 of sliced pitted Greek olives
- 6 large eggs
- 2 cups of fresh broccoli florets
- ¼ cup of 2% milk

Directions

1. Preheat the broiler ready.

2. Place a steamer basket over 1-in of water in a large sauce pan.
3. Place the broccoli in the basket.
4. Bring the water to boil.
5. Reduce the heat to allow it to simmer, steamed while covered in 4 – 6 minutes until crispy tender.
6. In another large bowl, whisk the eggs, salt, pepper, and milk.
7. Stir in the cooked broccoli, olives, and grated cheese.
8. Using a 10-in. over proof skillet, heat the oil over medium temperature.
9. Pour in the eggs.
10. Cook while uncovered for 4 – 6 minutes.
11. Broil 3 – 4-in form heat 2 – 4 minutes until when the eggs are totally set.
12. Let settle for 5 minutes.
13. Cut into wedges.
14. Sprinkle with shaved cheese and parsley.
15. Serve and enjoy

Tomato poached halibut

Ingredients

- 4 lemon wedges
- 1/3 cup of chopped cilantro
- ¼ cups of chopped pitted green olives
- 3 minced garlic cloves
- 4 halibut fillets weighing 4 ounces each
- ¼ teaspoon of pepper
- 1/8 teaspoon of salt
- 1 can of no salt added drained diced tomatoes
- 2 finely chopped poblano peppers
- 1 small chopped onions
- 1 tablespoon of olive oil
- Crusty whole grain bread
- 1 can of fire roasted diced tomatoes

Directions

1. Using a larger nonstick skillet, start by heating oil over a medium temperature.
2. Add the poblano peppers and the chopped onions.
3. Cook and stir for up to 4 – 6 minutes until tender.
4. Stir in the tomatoes, pepper, garlic, olives and salt then bring to boil

5. Keep adjusting the heat to enable a proper simmer.
6. Add the filets.
7. Cook when covered for 8 – 10 minutes or until when the fish starts flaking when tapped with a fork.
8. Sprinkle with cilantro.
9. With lemon wedges, serve and if desired serve with bread
10. Enjoy

Quinoa tabbouleh

Ingredients

- ½ teaspoon pepper
- ½ teaspoon of salt
- ¼ cup of lemon juice
- 2 tablespoons of olive oil
- 1/3 cup of minced parsley
- 2 cups of water
- 1 can of black beans washed and drained; should be 15 ounces
- 1 cup of quinoa
- 1 small chopped sweet red pepper
- 1 small peeled and chopped cucumber

Directions

1. Put water to boil in a large saucepan.
2. Add the quinoa
3. Reduce the heat to allow it to simmer and to absorb the extra liquid for 12 – 15 minutes.
4. Remove the content from heat and fluff it with a fork.
5. Transfer to another bowl to allow complete cooling.
6. Introduce the cucumber, beans, parsley, and beans.

7. In a small bowl whisk all the remaining ingredients, then drizzle over the salad and toss to coat.
8. Refrigerate the content until it is chilled.
9. Serve and enjoy

Parmesan chicken with artichoke hearts

Ingredients

- 2 thinly sliced green onions
- 4 boneless skinless chicken breast 6 ounces
- 1 lemon equally cut into 8 slices
- ¼ cup of shredded parmesan cheese
- 2 chopped garlic cloves
- 1 medium coarsely chopped onions
- 3 teaspoons olive oil
- ½ teaspoon of pepper
- 2 cans of water-packed artichokes hearts properly drained (should be 14 ounces each)
- ½ teaspoon of dried thyme
- 1 teaspoon of dried crushed rosemary
- ½ cup of white wine

Directions

1. Begin by preheating the oven to 375°.
2. Place the chicken in a baking pan with a thin coated cooking spray.
3. Drizzle with 1 teaspoon of oil.

4. Mix the rosemary, peppers, and thyme then sprinkle half of the mixture over the chicken.
5. In a large bowl, combine onions, wine, garlic, artichokes hearts, remaining oil and mixture of herbs then toss to coat.
6. Arrange the chicken and sprinkle with cheese then top with lemon slices.
7. Roast the content until the thermometer reads 165° in 20 – 25 minutes.
8. Evenly sprinkle with green onions
9. Serve

Creamy feta-spinach dip

This recipe can turn out to be more addictive and powerful dip because of the garlic and feta ingredients.

Do not worry, the addictiveness is due to the irresistibility delicious tasted the keep one hooked to continuously keep longing for more of it.

The ingredients and directions are shown below.

Ingredients

- Fresh vegetables
- 1 teaspoon of dill weed
- 1/8 teaspoon of pepper
- 1 minced garlic glove
- 1 cup of chopped fresh spinach
- ¼ cup of less fat sour cream
- 1 cup of fatless plain yogurt
- 2 ounces of fatless cubed cream cheese
- ¾ cup of crumbled feta cheese

Directions

1. Using a four layered cheesecloth, place is above a bowl.
2. Put yogurt in the prepared four layered cheesecloth o strainer.
3. Cover the edges of the yogurt with the cheesecloth.
4. Keeping it under refrigeration for about 2 hours to a point when the yogurt has completely thickened in a uniform manner to the whipped cream.
5. Transfer the yogurt to a food processor while the remaining liquid in the bowl can be discarded
6. Introduce the feta cheese, sour cream, garlic, cream cheese then cover it until content has completely smoothened.
7. Transfer to a small bowl where the spinach can then be stirred with the dill and pepper.
8. Cover and refrigerate until when chilled.
9. Serve with the vegetable and enjoy the taste.

Rice pilaf with apples and raisins

Ingredients

- 1/8 teaspoon of cayenne pepper
- ¼ teaspoon of ground allspice
- ¼ teaspoon of dried thyme
- 1 teaspoon of salt
- ¼ teaspoon of ground cinnamon
- 1 cup of water
- 2 tablespoons of olive oil
- ¼ cup of golden raisin
- 1 cup of uncooked jasmine rice
- 1 small chopped onion
- ¼ cup of chopped apples

Directions

1. Using a large saucepan, heat the oil over a medium temperature.
2. Sauté onions until when they become tender in 4 – 6 minutes.
3. Add the rice, then cook and stir until when the rice turns brown in about 4 – 6 minutes.
4. Introduce in the remaining ingredients and bring to boil.

5. Reduce the heat to allow it to simmer when covered to absorb the liquid until the rice is tender in 15 – 20 minutes.
6. Fluff with a fork
7. Serve

Mediterranean chicken

The preparation of this recipe is quite simple, yet heavy and irresistibly delicious in taste particularly when dressed with tomatoes, capers and olives.

This is a real knockout dish for several individuals and families.

Ingredients

- 1 pint of grape tomatoes
- 3 tablespoons of drained capers
- ¼ teaspoon of salt
- 3 tablespoon of olive oil
- ¼ teaspoon of peppers
- 16 pitted ripe sliced Greek olives
- 4 boneless skinless chicken breast which should be approximately 6 ounces each when halved

Directions

1. Ultimately, start the cooking by sprinkling the chicken with pepper and salt.
2. In an ovenproof large skillet, cook in the oil over a medium temperature until when it turns to golden brown in about 2 – 3 minutes on every side.

3. Add the capers, tomatoes, and olives.
4. Bake while uncovered at about 475° until when the thermometer reading drops to 170° in 10 – 14 minutes.
5. Serve and enjoy

9 781802 777024